UNOFFICIAL

1,000
Magical Herbs
and Fungi

1,000 Magical Herbs and Fungi

by James A. C. Muggleton

Publisher: Spell Book Shop

First Printing: 2016

ISBN 9781086184402

Spell Book Shop
http://www.facebook.com/SpellBookShop/

Forward

This book is an encyclopedia of potion ingredients from the Wizarding World of Harry Potter and references much of the mythology of that creation. The research which has gone into this volume has been quite extensive, utilizing sources such as the Wizarding World novels, movies, games and other mediums. From this point forward this work will refer to ingredients and magic from the fictitious wizarding world as if it was real; but rest assured that no such world really exists. It is simply the works and universe as created and presented by J. K. Rowling, noted author and philanthropist. If such as world was real, secret and hidden then this book wouldn't be in your hands at all and you would know absolutely nothing about it.

Here you'll find a botanical A-Z of magical herbs and fungi for easy plant identification and application. It is an essential tool in understanding both potion making and herbology, and as such, should be maintained as required texts for both sets of curricula throughout magical study. Although titled "Magical Herbs and Fungi," within this text you will find a wide variety of potion ingredients beyond those of the plant kingdom. In fact, after the chapter on magical herbs and fungi, the entire 2nd section of this book is dedicated to brief descriptions of potion ingredients that come from the animal kingdom, chemicals and minerals. Simply stated, this book's original title of "1,000 Magical Herbs and Fungi and Wings and Feathers and Eyeballs and Teeth and Stones and Other Classifications of Magical Ingredients" proved to be quite a mouthful, thus this shorter title is adequate. Please note that this volume does not include all one thousand different varieties of herbs and fungi found in the magical world, this book only includes the most important and interesting plants and fungi that would be useful to students and teachers.

*Lastly, it is absolutely essential to note that many of these ingredients, whether found in a potioneer's stock or out in the wild, **<u>can truly be poisonous and should not be handled</u>** without the proper magical guidance, protection and care. Wizards and witches in all stations and walks of life can benefit by keeping their copy of this book handy, as it contains the essence of our understanding of the magical world and acts as a crucial reference guide to potion ingredients.*

Preface

Herbology is the study of magical and mundane plants and fungi. Herbology is a core class and subject taught at any wizarding school in which students learn to care for and utilize plants. Students also learn about the magical properties of plants and what they are used for. Many plants provide ingredients for potions and medicine while others have magical effects of their own right. The further into a student's education, the more difficult and dangerous the plants become. An herbologist is a wizard or witch who is a specialist in the field of herbology.

Throughout her life, Headmistress Spore continued her work and research in herbology and worked with many noted wizarding and muggle biologists in cataloging her work. For example, her work with Carl Linnaeus helped to establish what is now known as biological kingdoms, including the animalia, plantae and fungi kingdoms. These classifications have been included in this textbook and updated as necessary to match the classifications of today's world. Within these classifications, the term "order" and the suffix "-anae" were developed by Armen Takhtajan.

The Kingdom Plantae (or plant) is divided into two groups: vascular and nonvascular plants. The many species of organisms in the Plant Kingdom are divided into several phyla, or divisions, totaling about 260,000 species of seed plants. Green plants provide a substantial proportion of the world's molecular oxygen and are the basis of most of Earth's ecologies, especially on land.

A fungus (plural: fungi) is any member of the group of eukaryotic organisms that includes microorganisms such as yeasts and molds, as well as the more familiar mushrooms. These organisms are classified in the kingdom fungi. Abundant worldwide, most fungi are inconspicuous because of the small size of their structures and their cryptic lifestyles in soil or on dead matter. They may become noticeable when fruiting, either as mushrooms or as molds. Fungi perform an essential role in the decomposition of organic matter and have fundamental roles in nutrient cycling and exchange in the environment.

Definitions

Conifer – a tree that bears cones and evergreen needles or scale-like leaves (such as cedar, cypress, fir, juniper, pine and redwood.)

Deciduous – a tree or shrub that sheds it's leaves annually (such as aspen, birch, elm maple or oak.)

Dioecious – a tree with separate male and female plants.

Drupe (Stone Fruit) – a fruit with a fleshy exterior which contains a hard pit where a seed is encased.

Herbaceous – a plant with no persistent woody stem above ground.

Herbaria – a collection of plants and data compiled for study. These are typically flattened plants kept in a book.

Nectar – a sugary fluid secreted by plants.

Nectary – the part of the flower that secrets nectar.

Plant Life Cycle – This includes a seed which germinated and grows into a plant. The plant then produces flowers which, when fertilized, produces more seeds in a fruit or seed pod. The plant eventually dies, leaving the seeds to produce new plants.

    Annual – a plant that completes its life cycle within one year.

    Biennials – a plan that takes two years to complete its life cycle.

    Perennial – a plant that lives for more than two years.

Polymorpha – an organism, usually a fungus, that can grow into many different shapes.

Stamen – the fertilizing part of a flower, usually containing pollen.

Stolon – a stem that connects separately from the flowering stem.

Subcosmopolitan/Cosmopolitan – an organism that is found across most or all the known world.

Table of Contents:

Section 2 - Potion Ingredients 65

Section 1

Magical Herbs
and Fungi

Aconite

Kingdom	Order	Family	Genus
Plantae	Ranunculales	Ranunculaceae	Aconitum

Native Region: Once widespread, aconite is mostly grown in the wild in Scotland. The species of aconite labeled chasmanthum, heterophyllum and vuilaceum are considered endangered.

Features: Most common blue-purple in color but can vary widely. The petals, leaves and roots are very toxic. Death usually occurs within two to six hours.

Magical Properties: Alertness, brevity, relaxation, calmness and awareness.

Details: Aconitum includes over 250 species, which include aconite, monkshood and wolf's bane. Aconitum species are highly toxic, although they have been used sparsely in medicine as a pain-reliever, diuretic, heart sedative, and to induce sweating.

Alihotsy

Kingdom	Order	Family	Genus
Magicae Plantae	Malvales	Malvaceae	Alihotum

Native Region: The island of Madagascar off the coast of east Africa.

Features: A thin tree with pink flowers; the leaves of the plant can be used to cause laughter.

Magical Properties: Induces hysteria and uncontrollable laughter.

Details: The name of the plant is derived from a Sidiki word meaning "lightness of spirit." Alihotsy is also known as the hyena tree. The leaves' mirth-inducing properties can be damaged by stirring it too vigorously while potion making.

Ammoniacum

Kingdom	Order	Family	Genus
Plantae	Apiales	Apiaceae	Ferula

Native Region: Deserts of Iran and mountains of Afghanistan.

Features: Ammoniacum has a faintly fetid, unpleasant odor; externally it possesses a reddish-yellow appearance and a waxy luster.

Magical Properties: Strong odor and digestive aid.

Details: Ammoniacum is a gum-resin exuded from the stem of a perennial herb in the apiceae family.

Angel's Trumpet

Kingdom	Order	Family	Genus
Plantae	Solanales	Solanaceae	Brugmansia

Native Region: Brugmansia is native to tropical South America in the Andes Mountains as well as southeastern Brazil.

Features: Woody shrubs with hanging (pendulous) flowers. The flowers typically are yellow, orange, pink or white. Although the entire plant is poisonous, the seeds and leaves are especially dangerous.

Magical Properties: Narcotic and highly poisonous. Anesthetic (loss of feeling) and anticholinergic (blocks nerve transmitters) properties.

Details: Also known as white thorn-apple, angel's trumpet is a genus of flowering plants. This plant is often used as a decoration in the west.

Arnica

Kingdom	Order	Family	Genus
Plantae	Asterales	Asteraceae	Arnica

Native Region: Europe.

Features: Long yellow petals with green stems covered in spreading hairs. The roots are usually unbranched. The plant has a strong sage odor.

Magical Properties: Healing of sprains and bruises.

Details: Arnica is a perennial, herbaceous plant. It is also poisonous is ingested in large quantities.

Asphodel

Kingdom	Order	Family	Genus
Plantae	Asparagales	Asphodelaceae	Asphodelus

Native Region: Central Spain and southwest France.

Features: From the lily family, this plant has long, slender leaves.

Magical Properties: Depending on the combination the root can be used to increase an individual's energy or decrease energy.

Details: Asphodel is a relative of the lily and native to Europe. The ancient Greeks associated it with the death and the underworld, believing there was a meadow of asphodel in Elysian Fields, and considered it sacred to Persephone, goddess of the spring and queen of the underworld. Asphodel was once believed to be a favorite food of the dead, and so was commonly planted near graves.

Balm

Kingdom	Order	Family	Genus
Plantae	Lamiales	Lamiaceae	Melissa

Native Region: Europe and Asia.

Features: Balm is a genus of perennial herbs that has leaves with a characteristic lemony smell. The leaves are ovate or heart-shaped.

Magical Properties: Healing and soothing.

Details: Balm, also known as lemon balm in the United States, is named Melissa from the Greek word meaning "honeybee" due to the large amount of nectar found in the plant's flowers.

Baneberry

Kingdom	Order	Family	Genus
Plantae	Ranunculales	Ranunculaceae	Actaea

Native Region: Alaska

Features: Although the entire plant is poisonous, the red and white berries from actaea rubra are particularly toxic and can cause nausea and dizziness or even death. The roots, though also poisonous can be used to reduce cramping.

Magical Properties: Poisonous, pestilence defense.

Details: Baneberry, also known as actaea rubra or "Herb Christopher" in England, is believed to ward off plague, insects, and vermin although it also attracts toads.

Bdellium Tree

Kingdom	Order	Family	Genus
Plantae	Sapindales	Burseraceae	Commiphora

Native Region: Commiphora wightii is commonly found in northern India and while commiphora africana is found in Africa.

Features: The commiphora trees secretes an aromatic gum-like myrrh called bdellion (bdelium) which is used for magical purposes. The leaves are trifoliate while the flowers are red and pink. The berries from the tree are red.

Magical Properties: Cleansing and strength.

Details: The bdellium tree is a shrub, growing no taller than 4 meters (13 feet) with thorny branches.

Belladonna (Deadly Nightshade)

Kingdom	Order	Family	Genus
Plantae	Solanales	Solanaceae	Atropa

Native Region: Temperate southern and central Europe.

Features: One of the most toxic plants of Europe. The seed of the belladonna plant is purple.

Magical Properties: Lightness, hallucination and flight.

Details: Other names for belladonna are atropa, deadly nightshade, death's herb, dwale, and witch's berry. The antidotes are the synthesized chemicals, physostigmine or pilocarpine.

Bloodroot

Kingdom	Order	Family	Genus
Plantae	Ranunculales	Papaveraceae	Sanguinaria

Native Region: North America amongst woods near flood plains.

Features: The petals are white with yellow stamens. The sap can be orange or red and is highly poisonous.

Magical Properties: Poison and antibiotic.

Details: Bloodroot, also known as sanguinaria, bloodwort, redroot and red puccoon, is a perennial flowering plant and its extract kills animal cells. Thus, internal use is inadvisable.

Boom Berry

Kingdom	Order	Family	Genus
Magicae Plantae	Rosales	Rosaceae	Rubus

Native Region: England and France.

Features: The red fruit of this subspecies of rubus plant causes a snap like sensation when crushed or chewed.

Magical Properties: Restoration, healing and alertness.

Details: Due to the popularity of the boom berry it was once considered a delight to find this plant growing wild. Today it is cultivated mostly in private wizarding gardens and is common in potion making.

Bubotuber

Kingdom	Order	Family	Genus
Magicae Plantae	Poales	Bromeliaceae	Satoposis

Native Region: Central and South America.

Features: The bubotuber features a long green tentacle shaped with pustules forming along the shaft. Bubotubers produce a pus that is valuable for its acne-ridding qualities. The pus is a thick, yellowish-green liquid and smells strongly of petrol.

Magical Properties: Irritant, antibacterial and cleansing.

Details: Despite retaining healing powers, when undiluted it can cause painful, large, yellow boils to form immediately on the skin, and dragon-hide gloves are recommended to be worn while handling it. It is an excellent remedy for the more severe cases of acne. These properties were discovered by Sacharissa Tugwood, who also created some of the earliest beautifying potions.

Bursting Mushroom

Kingdom	Order	Family	Genus
Magicae Fungi	Agaricales	Amanitaceae	Bondanita

Native Region: Scotland.

Features: White stalk and red and white-spotted cap.

Magical Properties: Fire resistance.

Details: When approached, a bursting mushroom will swell and shrink rapidly before violently exploding. One must be careful when harvesting this plant to avoid serious burns.

Castor Oil

Kingdom	Order	Family	Genus
Plantae	Malpighiales	Euphorbiaceae	Ricinus

Native Region: Mediterranean Region, Eastern Africa and India.

Features: The castor oil tree has glossy leaves containing green pigment. It produces a spiny fruit which contains a dark bean from which castor oil can be extracted.

Magical Properties: Food grade castor oil is a preservative and can be used to agitate and provoke.

Details: Also known as ricinus communis, castor oil has a long, unpleasant history of being used as punishment. This practice is highly discouraged, as it has been known to cause death.

Centaury

Kingdom	Order	Family	Genus
Plantae	Gentianales	Gentianaceae	Centaurium

Native Region: Europe and western Asia.

Features: Small pink flower with triangular leaves.

Magical Properties: Healing, friendliness and internal organ strength.

Details: Centaurium erythraea, also known as centaury, is an erect biennial herb.

Cherry

Kingdom	Order	Family	Genus
Plantae	Rosales	Rosaceae	Prunus

Native Region: Turkey, northern Europe and Asia.

Features: A cherry is a fleshy drupe, usually consisting of two small red fruits, each having their own stems connected by a small tip at the top.

Magical Properties: Invisibility and happiness.

Details: The branches or wood of cherry tree is also used in making wands.

Chilli (Chili Pepper)

Kingdom	Order	Family	Genus
Plantae	Solanales	Solanaceae	Capsicum

Native Region: Mexico

Features: The fruit of the capsicum. It can be green, red or yellow.

Magical Properties: Increase body temperature, decrease pain.

Details: A popular fruit to use in cooking due to the spicy flavoring. The magical properties have proven to be useful in both humans and beasts, particularly in dragons who suffer from Squabbs Syndrome.

Chinese Chomping Cabbage

Kingdom	Order	Family	Genus
Magicae Plantae	Brassicales	Brassicaceae	Brassica

Native Region: China

Features: Dense leafy green plant that will chomp on nearby objects.

Magical Properties: Increase bone density and strength.

Details: Contains healthy portions of calcium and vitamin K making it healthy for culinary use, although traditional cabbage is somewhat easier to tame.

Cinnamon

Kingdom	Order	Family	Genus
Plantae	Laurales	Lauraceae	Cinnamomum

Native Region: India, Sri Lanka, Bangladesh and Myanmar.

Features: Cinnamon is used for potion making in stick form or powder.

Magical Properties: Increases charisma and induces calm.

Details: Cinnamon is a spice obtained from the inner bark of several trees from the genus Cinnamomum that is used in both sweet and savory foods.

Comfrey

Kingdom	Order	Family	Genus
Plantae	Boraginales	Boraginaceae	Symphytum

Native Region: Ireland and Britain in damp, grassy places.

Features: Comfrey has a black, turnip-like root and road leaves with bell-shaped flowers of cream or purple.

Magical Properties: When used topically, it can strengthen bone marrow and resolve skin issues.

Details: Essence of comfrey is the essential oil of comfrey, a plant used in organic gardening and herbal medicine.

Cornflower

Kingdom	Order	Family	Genus
Plantae	Asterales	Asteraceae	Centaurea

Native Region: Temperate Europe.

Features: Cornflower is an annual plant with gray-green branched stems and intense blue flowerheads that blooms all summer.

Magical Properties: Extract from cornflower is effective in easing tired eyes.

Details: Considered a beneficial weed, its edible flowers are used in tea blends. Cornflowers are worn by young men in love and if the flower fades quickly, it is taken as a sign that his love is not returned.

Cowbane

Kingdom	Order	Family	Genus
Plantae	Apiales	Apiaceae	Circuta

Native Region: Norther Europe and Asia.

Features: The roots are white and bulbous. The stems are smooth, branching and hollow. Flowers are white and clustered in an umbrella shape.

Magical Properties: Poison, destruction and shrinking.

Details: Also known as circuta virosa. The poison of cowbane can cause nausea, seizures and death. It can be confused with parsnip due to their similar features.

Daisy

Kingdom	Order	Family	Genus
Plantae	Asterales	Asteraceae	Aster

Native Region: Europe

Features: A daisy is a common wildflower with white, pink or yellow petals of various positioning. The roots can be a single dominant with fibrous offshoots.

Magical Properties: The petals can be used for color change while the root is used for shrinking.

Details: Daisies are often considered weeds because they thrive in inhospitable conditions and are resistant to bugs and even magical pesticides. The name daisy is derived from its Old English "dægesege" meaning "day's eye," because the petals open at dawn and close at dusk.

Dandelion

Kingdom	Order	Family	Genus
Plantae	Asterales	Asteraceae	Taraxacum

Native Region: Europe and southern Russia.

Features: Hollow green stem with a single flower at the top. The flower head is yellow with numerous petals. Dandelions also have a seed stage when the flower head is replaced with a seed head where the white, fluffy seeds form a dome shape.

Magical Properties: Healing and cures infections.

Details: Taraxaum or dandelion is a perennial, herbaceous plant that prefers temperate areas of the earth. Dandelion comes from French, meaning "lion's tooth." Though often considered a weed, the dandelion adds minerals and nitrogen to soil which benefits nearby plant life.

Deadlyius

Kingdom	Order	Family	Genus
Magicae Fungi	Agaricales	Amanitaceae	Amanita

Native Region: Forests of Europe.

Features: White stem and dome.

Magical Properties: Poisonous. If properly manipulated it can also enable dark magic detection.

Details: Deadlyius is often mixed among other mushrooms in the forests of Europe which make it difficult to differentiate from other poisonous plants such as fool's mushroom, which has no magical properties.

Dead Man's Fingers

Kingdom	Order	Family	Genus
Fungi	Xylariales	Xylariaceae	Xylaria

Native Region: Forest.

Features: Elongated, upright polymorpha.

Magical Properties: Healing and growth inhibitor.

Details: Xylaria polymorpha, or dead man's fingers, grows from the base of injured stumps or decaying wood. The inside of the brown fungus is white.

Death Cap

Kingdom	Order	Family	Genus
Fungi	Agaricales	Amanitaceae	Amaita

Native Region: Europe

Features: White stem and cap with green highlights.

Magical Properties: Poisonous and highly toxic.

Details: The death cap mushroom, or amanita phalloides, is believed to be the cause of most mushroom related poisonings worldwide, as it resembles edible mushrooms.

Devil's Snare

Kingdom	Order	Family	Genus
Magicae Plantae	Solanales	Solanales	Datura

Native Region: Mexico.

Features: Devil's snare is composed of a mass of soft, springy tendrils and vines that possess some sense of touch.

Magical Properties: The leaves of devil's snare is known to cause anxiety and can be toxic.

Details: Also known as datura stramonium, jimsonweed, thornapple or moon flower, devil's snare will usually maintain a height of only 2 to 5 feet and flower during the summer. With magical application the plan will transform into its much deadlier form with the magical ability to strangle anything near it. Struggling or resisting devil's snare will cause the plant to exert a greater force of constriction. If the victim can relax, the snare will relax its grip on them. Devil's snare in this form hates light from the sun.

Devil's Trumpet

Kingdom	Order	Family	Genus
Plantae	Solanales	Solanaceae	Datura

Native Region: Central America and Mexico.

Features: Herbaceous bush with erect flowers. Most have spines on their fruit. Although the entire plant is poisonous, the seeds and leaves are especially dangerous. The flowers can be white, yellow pale pink or pale purple.

Magical Properties: Poisonous, delirium, hyperthermia, amnesia and death.

Details: Datura is considered a "witches' weed" which also includes deadly nightshade, henbane and mandrake due to a long history of causing death.

Dittany

Kingdom	Order	Family	Genus
Plantae	Lamiales	Lamiaceae	Cunila

Native Region: Eastern United States.

Features: Late-summer flowering shrub with small purple flowers.

Magical Properties: Healing and restoration.

Details: In addition to being applied topically, the raw plant can be consumed to heal shallow wounds.

Extinguisher Moss

Kingdom	Order	Family	Genus
Plantae	Encalyptales	Encalyptaceae	Encalypta

Native Region: Subcosmopolitan.

Features: Small flowerless plant that grows in dense clumps or mats, often in shady locations. Does not contain seeds.

Magical Properties: When brewed into a fine mist, extinguisher moss has the ability to cover, veil or hide people or objects from view temporarily.

Details: Traditionally used as insulation and for the ability to absorb liquids up to twenty times its weight.

Fat Red Toadstool

Kingdom	Order	Family	Genus
Fungi	Agaricales	Amanitaceae	Amanita

Native Region: Temperate regions of northern Europe, northern Asia and North America.

Features: Large mushroom with a red dome and white dots.

Magical Properties: Causes a hypnotic state or delirium.

Details: Amanita muscarui, also known as fly agaric or simply fat red toadstool, is found in temperate regions. Although this plant is poisonous, deaths due to ingestion is uncommon. Fat red toadstool associates with various deciduous and coniferous trees.

Field Mushroom

Kingdom	Order	Family	Genus
Fungi	Agaricales	Agaricaceae	Agaricus

Native Region: Grassy areas following rainfall, subcosmopolitan.

Features: White cap mushroom with pink gills that turn red then brown over time.

Magical Properties: Healing of ulcers and bed sores.

Details: Agaricus campestris, also known as the field mushroom or meadow mushroom, is often confused with other poisonous mushrooms due to similar characteristics. Field mushrooms will often grow in groups organized in a wide ring shape.

Flitterbloom

Kingdom	Order	Family	Genus
Magicae Plantae	Solanales	Solanales	Datura

Native Region: North America.

Features: Flitterbloom is composed of a mass of soft, springy tendrils and vines that possess some sense of touch.

Magical Properties: Relaxation and calm.

Details: Flitterbloom is known for its magical ability to control or soften the mood within its environment. This has made the flitterbloom a popular household flowering plant. Although flitterbloom may resemble the darkened version of devil's snare, the flitterbloom is perfectly safe.

Fluxweed

Kingdom	Order	Family	Genus
Plantae	Brassiclaes	Brassicaceae	Descurainia

Native Region: Tropical and temperate Africa and Asia.

Features: The stem of fluxweed stands up straight with tiny green branches.

Magical Properties: Healing, restoration and reconstruction.

Details: Fluxweed is a member of the mustard family known for its healing properties. When picked at the full moon, fluxweed's healing properties become strong enough to completely restructure most any deformations.

Formatogoria

Kingdom	Order	Family	Genus
Magicae Plantae	Rosales	Rosaceae	Gracia

Native Region: France.

Features: The formatogoria has a single long stem with a large flower containing white, crystal-like petals. Smaller blue flowers bud along each branch.

Magical Properties: Increases the potency of ingredients it is combined with.

Details: Formatogoria, a perennial flowering plant, grows in the wild under unknown circumstances.

Foxglove

Kingdom	Order	Family	Genus
Plantae	Lamiales	Plantaginaceae	Digitalis

Native Region: Southwestern Europe.

Features: Tall green stalk with dropping, bell like flowers of varying colors such as pink, purple, yellow or white.

Magical Properties: Poisonous and causes bloating.

Details: Also known as dead man's bells and witch's gloves, all of the floxglove plant is toxic from the seed to the root. Ingesting foxglove can cause vomiting, seizures, yellowed vision or blurred vision.

Ginger

Kingdom	Order	Family	Genus
Plantae	Zingiberales	Zingiberaceae	Zingiber

Native Region: Tropical rainforest in southern Asia, and India.

Features: Reed-like plant with white and pink flower buds that bloom into yellow flowers. The roots are fibrous.

Magical Properties: The roots are used to increase concentration, comprehension and confidence.

Details: Although a popular spice, ginger is even more favored by potioneers for its group of positive magical properties. Ginger is no longer grown in the wild.

Gomas Barbadensis

Kingdom	Order	Family	Genus
Magicae Plantae	Fabales	Fabaceae	Bardadenae

Native Region: West Indies and tropical America.

Features: Flowering plant which produces a legume. The stalk is filled with a gummy residue.

Magical Properties: Ridiculously sticky substance.

Details: Gomas Barbadensis is often overlooked due to its resemblance to Caesalpinia, a similar flowering plant. The legume itself has no known magical properties.

Goosegrass

Kingdom	Order	Family	Genus
Plantae	Gentianales	Rubiaceae	Galium

Native Region: Europe, Asia and Africa.

Features: Annual plants with creeping stems that cover nearby terrain. The stem and leaves are covered with small hooking hairs to help them attach to objects.

Magical Properties: Cohesion of elements.

Details: Goosegrass, also known as galium aparine, cleavers, catchweed and stickyweed, spreads itself by sticking to animal fur. Although not a main potion ingredient itself, goosegrass is useful in most any potion as it helps other ingredients as they infuse together.

Gillyweed

Kingdom	Order	Family	Genus
Magicae Chromista	Laminariales	Chordaceae	Chorda

Native Region: Mediterranean Sea

Features: Green, slimy and wormlike.

Magical Properties: Enables one to grow gills.

Details: When it is eaten by a witch or wizard, one grows gills and webbing between the fingers and toes, allowing them to process oxygen from water and navigate underwater more easily. There is some debate among Herbologists as to the duration of the effects of gillyweed in fresh water versus salt water, but the effects of gillyweed in fresh water seem to last about an hour.

Hellebore

Kingdom	Order	Family	Genus
Plantae	Ranunculales	Ranunculaceae	Helleborus

Native Region: Europe and Asia.

Features: A five petal flower of white or pink which contain nectar in the center. Long green leaves extrude from the stem. When the nectar is extracted into a syrup it will turn blue.

Magical Properties: The leaves are poisonous. The processed syrup of hellebore can cause calmness and quietness.

Details: Hellebore is a flowering plant. The name derives from Greek, "food to injure." Due to the flower's soft colors, Hellebore is also known as winter rose, Christmas rose and lenten rose although it is not a rose.

Hemlock

Kingdom	Order	Family	Genus
Plantae	Apiales	Apiaceae	Conium

Native Region: Europe and north Africa.

Features: Small, white petal flowers with a hollow stem. The leaves are finely divided in small groups.

Magical Properties: Highly poisonous. It can severely weaken magical creatures.

Details: Conium Maculatum is a poisonous biennial herbaceous flowering plant from the carrot family. Hemlock is famous for being the poison that killed Socrates.

Henbane

Kingdom	Order	Family	Genus
Plantae	Solanales	Solanceae	Hyoscyamus

Native Region: Europe and Asia.

Features: Yellow petals with greenish-yellow leaves and sharp points at the tips.

Magical Properties: Sedative and poison.

Details: Hyoscyamus niger is also known as black henbane or stinking nightshade. It is historically known for its magical properties but also for its high toxicity.

Henna Tree

Kingdom	Order	Family	Genus
Plantae	Myrtales	Lythraceae	Lawsonia

Native Region: Tropical zones such as southern Asia, Australia and Africa.

Features: Henna is a tall shrub or small tree. The leaves grow opposite along the stem and the small flowers can be red or white.

Magical Properties: Black color dye.

Details: Lawsonia inermis, also known as hina, the mignonette tree, and the Egyptian privet, is a flowering plant. It is the source of the dye "henna." The henna tree is the only member of the lawsonia genus.

Itchweed

Kingdom	Order	Family	Genus
Plantae	Liliales	Melanthiaceae	Veratrum

Native Region: North America.

Features: Heavily ribbed leaves are spirally arranged and hairy on the underside. It also has numerous yellow-green flowers and the fruit holds the seeds like a capsule.

Magical Properties: Nausea, vomiting, cold sweat, vertigo.

Details: Veratrum virdide, also known as itchweed, grows in wet meadows, sunny streambanks and open forests. Extract from the itchweed root was used to treat high blood pressure until it was determined to be highly toxic and deadly.

Jewelweed

Kingdom	Order	Family	Genus
Plantae	Ericales	Balsaminaceae	Impatiens

Native Region: North America.

Features: Growing up to 5 feet tall with orange blooming flowers from late spring into the fall. The stems are a little translucent.

Magical Properties: Fungicide.

Details: Impatiens capensis, jewelweed or common jewelweed is an annual plant native to North America. It is commonly found in ditches or along creeks. Amongst a patch of the orange common jewelweed one may find the rare yellow jewelweed too.

Kelp

Kingdom	Order	Family	Genus
Protista	Laminariales	Laminariaceae	Saccharina

Native Region: Northern Atlantic and the northern Pacific.

Features: Long, brown laminae or a rather large size. Seaweed doesn't have roots although the parts used to anchor themselves to other objects may appear rootlike.

Magical Properties: Nutrition, tolerance and open-mindedness.

Details: Kelp is a type of seaweed. When dried, it can be used as an ingredient in potions such as fertilizer. It was used often in Japan for food before migrating to China.

Knotgrass

Kingdom	Order	Family	Genus
Plantae	Poales	Poaceae	Paspalum

Native Region: Tropical American continents.

Features: Grass which grows in clumps and can get as high as 60 cm.

Magical Properties: Regeneration, combination and bonding.

Details: Knotgrass is a perennial grass. Also known as, paspalum distichum, water finger-grass and eternity grass, knotgrass is a favorite food amongst birds but can also be very effective in a variety of potions.

Lady's Mantle

Kingdom	Order	Family	Genus
Plantae	Rosales	Rosaceae	Alchemilla

Native Region: Subarctic regions of Europe and Asia.

Features: Fan-shaped leaves with small teeth at the tips, covered in soft hairs that makes water bead on them. Petal-less and bright chartreuse.

Magical Properties: Attraction and hormone inducing.

Details: Lady's Mantle is a small herbaceous plant with about 300 species and is native to cool temperatures.

Lavender

Kingdom	Order	Family	Genus
Plantae	Lamiales	Lamiaceae	Lavandula

Native Region: Europe, Asia and Africa.

Features: The petals are most commonly violet or blue in color. The leaf shape can be simple or complex.

Magical Properties: Calming, languid and sleepiness.

Details: Lavender is an annual herbaceous plant with 47 species of flowering varieties. Many types of lavender are cultivated in temperate climates and use for their oils.

Leaping Toadstool

Kingdom	Order	Family	Genus
Magicae Fungi	Agaricales	Agaricaceae	Camericus

Native Region: Grasslands in Europe and North America.

Features: White steam and cap with green highlights.

Magical Properties: Adjusts the muscles and ligaments to allow a higher tolerance of physical exertion.

Details: A leaping toadstool has the ability to jump. The toadstool will retain this attribute long after being picked so maintain caution when cooking or using in a potion, since this ingredient may leap out of a cauldron at any moment.

Lemongrass

Kingdom	Order	Family	Genus
Plantae	Poales	Poaceae	Cymbopogon

Native Region: Tropical Asia, Australia and Africa.

Features: Green grass growing about 2 m (6.6 ft) high with a soft citrus flavor.

Magical Properties: Repel insect or attract honey bees. The oil can be used to soften texture or add a citrus scent.

Details: Also known as silky heads, fever grass and barbed wire grass, it can be used in potions fresh, dried or powdered.

Lichen

Kingdom	Order	Family	Genus
Fungi	Lecanorales	Pannariaceae	Various

Native Region: Subcosmopolitan

Features: Variety of size, shapes and colors.

Magical Properties: The lichen will duplicate the magical effect of the fungus it is grown on.

Details: A lichen is the combination of algae amongst a fungus. Lichens can be mossy (such as wolf lichen), leaf-like, crusty or powdery.

Lily

Kingdom	Order	Family	Genus
Plantae	Liliales	Liliaceae	Lilium

Native Region: Temperate Europe and Asia.

Features: White, curled petals with protruding yellow stamens. The green stem sprouts from a bulb.

Magical Properties: Restores happiness after loss.

Details: Perennial, herbaceous flowering plant that grows from bulbs. Lilies are anciently revered and popular as they are considered to be tied to motherhood and divinity.

Ling

Kingdom	Order	Family	Genus
Plantea	Ericales	Ericaceae	Calluna

Native Region: Europe and Asia.

Features: Small leaves with many small purple flowers.

Magical Properties: Antiseptic, detoxifier and anti-inflammatory.

Details: Ling, also known as heather, is a low-growing shrub. It is the only species in the genus calluna.

Lovage

Kingdom	Order	Family	Genus
Plantae	Apiales	Apiaceae	Levisticum

Native Region: Europe and Asia.

Features: Tall, thin plant with stems sprouting green, jagged leaves. The flowers at the top are green or yellowish. The dry fruit breaks down into two parts.

Magical Properties: Inflammation, confusion and befuddlement.

Details: Lovage is an erect, herbaceous, perennial plant, similar to celery, whose fruit and seeds are used in cooking. It has been used in herbal medicines for centuries, especially to facilitate digestion. The plant matures in autumn.

Mallowsweet

Kingdom	Order	Family	Genus
Magicae Plantae	Santalales	Santalaceae	Santalum

Native Region: Oceana such as Australia, Hawaii and the Chinese islands.

Features: Woody flowering plant, with a strong herbal scent.

Magical Properties: Aids in divination and causes hallucinations. Very dangerous.

Details: The roots of mallowsweet photosynthesize nourishment but connects to other plants for water and inorganic nutrients like a parasite. Mallowsweet is also an herb that Centaurs burn to observe the fumes and flames to refine the results of their stargazing.

Mandrake

Kingdom	Order	Family	Genus
Plantae	Solanales	Solanaceae	Mandragora

Native Region: Mediterranean.

Features: Large brown roots that looks like a human and leaves that form a rosette with purple streaks. The berries are yellow or orange.

Magical Properties: Leaves causes transformations or sedation. The roots are used for restoration.

Details: Perennial herbaceous plant which, when matured, can be fatal to any person who hears the cry from its roots. If not fully grown, the scream merely renders a person unconscious. As a mandrake matures it mimics the live patterns of nearby species. Both dugbogs and flesh-eating slugs favor mandrakes.

Mastic Tree

Kingdom	Order	Family	Genus
Plantae	Sapindales	Anacardiaceae	Pistacia

Native Region: Mediterranean.

Features: Evergreen shrub with dioecious plants. The green leaves come in five or six pairs per branch. The fruit starts off red then blackens as it ripens.

Magical Properties: The resin from the tree causes gas in the gastrointestinal tract.

Details: The mastic tree is resistant to frost and can grow in any type of soil. As the tree ages, the trunk thickens and produces longer branches. The resin from the mastic tree is smelly and ivory colored.

Mint

Kingdom	Order	Family	Genus
Plantae	Lamiales	Lamiaceae	Mentheae

Native Region: Subcosmopolitan.

Features: Multiple stems of green leaves arranged in symmetric pairs. Mint can grow up to 4 feet (1.2 meters) and spread indefinitely. The fruit contains up to four seeds.

Magical Properties: Healing and restoration. Peppermint also strengthens resolve and self-control.

Details: Mint is a genus of strongly scented herbs. They thrive near water and can exist in a wide variety of conditions. Popular types include peppermint, spearmint, cornmint and apple mint.

Mistletoe Berries

Kingdom	Order	Family	Genus
Plantae	Santalales	Santalaceae	Viscum

Native Region: Europe.

Features: Mistletoe contains many small branches that produce rounded or sharp evergreen leaves. The berries are small, white and waxy.

Magical Properties: Leaves are very poisonous, causing convulsions, forgetfulness or death. In some brews, small portions of the berries can be used as a cure for common poisons.

Details: Mistletoe grows on host trees. As the seeds spread, the growth causes prosthesis itself and eventually depends on the attached tree to continue its growth. Mistletoe has been known to overcome and at times even kill part or the entire the host tree.

Moly

Kingdom	Order	Family	Genus
Magicae Plantae	Asparagales	Amaryllidaceae	Galanthus

Native Region: South Western Europe.

Features: Moly plants are easily recognized by their distinctive black stems and white flowers.

Magical Properties: Moly is powerful plant with many powerful properties: Moly plants are known to protect against Dark Enchantments, and can be eaten to counteract them.

Details: Also known as snowdrops, they are among the first bulbs to bloom in spring and can form impressive carpets of white in areas where they thrive.

Moondew

Kingdom	Order	Family	Genus
Magicae Plantae	Lamiales	Lamiaceae	Cliodna

Native Region: Scotland.

Features: Fibrous roots with dark green leaves containing red veins with jagged edges.

Magical Properties: Revival, awaken and restore.

Details: The magical properties of Moondew were discovered by druidess Cliodna in the Middle Ages. Moondew is used in potion making in liquid form.

Moonseed

Kingdom	Order	Family	Genus
Plantae	Ranunculales	Menispermaceae	Menispermum

Native Region: North America or northeastern Asia.

Features: Moonseed is a vine with clusters of small berries, which seeds resemble a crescent moon.

Magical Properties: Poisonous.

Details: Menisoerumum is Greek for "moonseed." There are only 3 species of moonseed which grows in moist woods and by streams.

Motherwort

Kingdom	Order	Family	Genus
Plantae	Lamiales	Lamiaceae	Leonurus

Native Region: Southeastern Europe and Central Asia.

Features: The stem has short hairs with branches holding leaves with three points. Multiple flowers decorate the top half of the plant. The petals are pink.

Magical Properties: Healing and disinfectant.

Details: Motherwort is an herbaceous perennial plant of the mint family. Other common names include throw-wort, lion's ear and lion's tail.

Neem

Kingdom	Order	Family	Genus
Plantae	Sapindales	Meliaceae	Azadirachta

Native Region: India.

Features: Evergreen tree with thin branches and a dense crown of thin leaves. The flowers are white and fragrant. The fruit is a yellowish droupe.

Magical Properties: Repel inspects and fungus. Antibacterial.

Details: The seeds of the fruit produced neem oil. The tree grows swiftly and is fairly drought resistant.

Niffler's Fancy

Kingdom	Order	Family	Genus
Magicae Plantae	Sapindales	Anacardiaceae	Pecunia

Native Region: North America.

Features: It has gleaming leaves that shine like copper.

Magical Properties: Rare and unknown.

Details: The shiny leaves of this plant are known to have been used as one of the earliest forms of wizarding currency, by primitive wizards. Perhaps because of this, niffler's fancy is a rare plant nowadays. It has not been well studied as a potion ingredient; however, it is known that it is a powerfully magical potion ingredient, since it is one of the constituents of the Potion of All Potential.

Nightshade

Kingdom	Order	Family	Genus
Plantae	Solanales	Solanaceae	Solanum

Native Region: Subcosmopolitan.

Features: The solanaceae family of plants are wide and varied, from trees and shrubs to vines and epiphytes. They often produce white flowers that bloom in all seasons except for winter.

Magical Properties: Some Solanaceae, like tomatoes, potatoes and eggplant are very healthy, opposed to deadly nightshade (or atropa belladonna) which can have very unpredictable, poisonous effects.

Details: Due to the variety of the nightshade family, and the confusion with deadly nightshade, it is important to be aware that most of the nightshade family are used in everyday life.

Nutmeg

Kingdom	Order	Family	Genus
Plantae	Magnoliales	Myristicaceae	Myristica

Native Region: Spice Islands in Indonesia.

Features: Myristica fragrans is a small evergreen tree reaching as high as 20m (66 ft) tall. The flowers are bell-shaped and yellow. The fruit is orange and contains a brown pit that contains nutmeg.

Magical Properties: The seed covering (aril) produces a spice called mace which induces confidence, smugness or arrogance. Nutmeg from the seed of the plant is known to increase cheer, modestly and goodwill.

Details: Nutmeg, also known as nux myristica, must be used in small doses to avoid hallucinogenic effects. After nutmeg is ground up, it will lose its flavor and magical effect quickly.

Olibanum (Frankincense)

Kingdom	Order	Family	Genus
Plantae	Sapindales	Burseraceae	Boswellia

Native Region: Arabian Peninsula and northeastern Africa.

Features: Small deciduous tree with smooth bark. Its flowers are yellow while the fruit is small and round.

Magical Properties: The oil from the bark gives off a sweet scent.

Details: Olibanum, also known as Frankincense, is an aromatic resin obtained from trees of the genus Boswellia. Olibanum is usually burnt as incense. The trees start producing resin when they are about 8 to 10 years old.

Onion

Kingdom	Order	Family	Genus
Plantae	Asparagales	Amaryllidaceae	Allium

Native Region: Asia.

Features: The onion plant has a series of hollow, turquoise leaves and its bulb grows underground, surrounded by a flakey skin.

Magical Properties: Healing and restoration.

Details: Freshly cut onions often cause a stinging sensation in the eyes of people nearby, and often uncontrollable tears. Onions are toxic to dogs, cats and many other animals.

Oppopanax (Myrrh)

Kingdom	Order	Family	Genus
Plantae	Sapindales	Burseraceae	Commiphora

Native Region: Subtropical Africa and Arabian Peninsula.

Features: Oppopanax has a reddish-brown color and a pleasant aroma.

Magical Properties: Perfume and increased immunity. Spirit of Myrrh is an antibiotic.

Details: Oppopanax, or opobalsam, is an oil extracted from the commiphora erythraea species of plant. When a tree wound penetrates through the bark and into the sapwood, the tree bleeds a resin. Myrrh gum, like frankincense, is such a resin.

Orchids

Kingdom	Order	Family	Genus
Plantae	Asparagales	Orchidaceae	Orchis

Native Region: Cosmopolitan

Features: The petals come in many variations of color and shape. Orchids will have two or three stamens.

Magical Properties: Enhances awareness and insight.

Details: Orchids are a flowering plant known for the color and vibrancy of their blooms. As one of the largest families of flowering plants, there are about 28 thousand species of orchids. The family of orchidaceae also includes the vanilla plant, though it is not known for any magical properties.

Peony

Kingdom	Order	Family	Genus
Plantae	Saxifragales	Paeoniaceae	Paeonia

Native Region: Asia, southern Europe and northwestern America.

Features: Compound, pointed leaves with fragrant flowers. The colors span from pink, white or yellow.

Magical Properties: The roots reduce convulsions. The petals cause shame or bashfulness.

Details: An herbaceous perennial plant, the peony is among the longest used flowers in Eastern culture. It is known as the "king of the flowers." If a plant is relocated it will take several years before it will bloom again.

Peruvian Pepper

Kingdom	Order	Family	Genus
Plantae	Sapindales	Anacardiaceae	Schinus

Native Region: Northern South America.

Features: Quick growing evergreen tree with upper branches that tend to droop. The fruit has woody seeds that turn from green to red, pink or purplish and can have hundreds of berries in dense clusters. The rough grayish bark is twisted and drips sap.

Magical Properties: Removes the effects of other toxins.

Details: Schinus molle, or Peruvian pepper, has bark, leaves and berries that are aromatic when crushed. The sweet outer part of ripe fruit can be used to make a drink or be boiled down into a syrup.

Plangentine

Kingdom	Order	Family	Genus
Magicae Plantae	Sapindales	Rutaceae	Plangentora

Native Region: Northern Europe and northern Asia.

Features: The plangent tree is more drought tolerant than the light blue fruit. The plangentine is tender and is damaged easily by heat.

Magical Properties: Comfort and tranquility.

Details: Although the tree grows year-round, the plangentine fruit is produced during the winter. If the fruit it picked during moonlight, the magical effect is more potent.

Plantain

Kingdom	Order	Family	Genus
Plantae	Zingiberales	Musaceae	Musa

Native Region: Southeast Asia.

Features: Long, curved fruit that grows in clusters with light green skin. They turn yellow as they ripen. The leaves can grow to over 2 meters (6.5 feet).

Magical Properties: Healing and muscle strength.

Details: Also known as cooking bananas, plantains grow on herbaceous plants called musa. Plantains are similar to bananas, only firmer and starchier. The fruit grows year-round.

Poison Ivy

Kingdom	Order	Family	Genus
Plantae	Sapindales	Anacardiaceae	Toxicodendron

Native Region: North America.

Features: Poison ivy can be a vine or a shrub with woody stems. The deciduous leaves protrude in threes from the branches with colors ranging from red, orange, yellow and green.

Magical Properties: Poisonous and allergic reactions.

Details: Poison ivy is the common name of toxicodendron radicans, a poisonous flowering plant known for the production of a fluid that causes skin irritation.

Polypodium (Polypody)

Kingdom	Order	Family	Genus
Plantae	Polypodiales	Polypodiaceae	Polypodium

Native Region: Tropical regions.

Features: A fern with large, divided leaves called fronds. The spore cases grow from the fronds.
Magical Properties: The juice extract causes the body to dispel toxins.

Details: The name polypdium is Greek for "little foot." There are about 100 fern species in this genus with a variety of nicknames.

Pomegranate

Kingdom	Order	Family	Genus
Plantae	Myrtales	Lythraceae	Punica

Native Region: Southeastern Asia.

Features: A shrub or small tree growing up to 10 meters (33 feet) high with spiny branches. The flower petals are red. The fruit is maroon and contains hundreds of edible seeds.

Magical Properties: The juice of the pomegranate is used for focus and concentration.

Details: Pomegranate trees have been known to live for hundreds of years.

Poppy

Kingdom	Order	Family	Genus
Plantae	Ranunculales	Papaveraceae	Papaver

Native Region: Europe.

Features: The plant has a greyish-green appearance and the stem and leaves are sparsely covered with coarse hairs. The flowering petals are white or red.

Magical Properties: Causes jovial or careless actions.

Details: Flowering plant with species that include morphine in dangerous levels. Some of the more benign seeds contain minimal content and can be found in a variety of dishes. Poppies have been the cause of wars amongst muggle populations.

Preacher's Porridge

Kingdom	Order	Family	Genus
Magicae Plantae	Caryophyllales	Droseraceae	Padmaea

Native Region: North America.

Features: Thorny plant with bulbus tips that connect to white pods. Each pod contains a blue, lumpy slime which constitutes the porridge part of the plant.

Magical Properties: Rare and unknown.

Details: Preacher's porridge is an aquatic plant although it can grow in almost any environment. The pods attract small bugs which can be captured to produce the blue slime.

Puffapod

Kingdom	Order	Family	Genus
Magicae Plantae	Proteales	Nelumbonaceae	Runabo

Native Region: Tropical Asia and Australia.

Features: Pink pods containing shining beans.

Magical Properties: Replication and duplication.

Details: The puffapod was a magical plant that produces large pink seedpods full of shining beans, which instantly flower when they come into contact with any solid object. Trolls are allergic to puffapods.

Pungous Onion

Kingdom	Order	Family	Genus
Plantae	Asparagales	Amaryllidaceae	Allium

Native Region: Asia.

Features: Pungous onion is a magical plant comprised of a swathe of green leaves and an orange elongated bulb at the base.

Magical Properties: Healing and regeneration. The pungous onion is known to be much more potent than other onions.

Details: Pungous onions are very pungent with a strong onion smell. Contact with freshly chopped pungous onions can be very dangerous as the juice can cause a serious burning sensation.

Quassia Amara

Kingdom	Order	Family	Genus
Plantae	Sapindales	Simaroubaceae	Quassia

Native Region: Central America and northern South America.

Features: A particularly drought tolerant shrub or small tree with large winged leaflets and bright red flowers which are white on the inside. The fruit is a small drupe.

Magical Properties: Extracts from the wood effectively repel large insects and spiders.

Details: Quassia amara, also known as amargo, bitter-ash or hombre grande, is one of the most bitter substances found in nature. It can also be used to treat fevers and kill pests.

Rose

Kingdom	Order	Family	Genus
Plantae	Rosales	Rosaceae	Rosa

Native Region: Mostly Asia with some species native to North America, Europe and Africa.

Features: The stem stands erect and is covered with sharp thorns. The flower petals come in a variety of different colors.

Magical Properties: The thorns cause feelings of dependency and infatuation. The petals create allure and charm.

Details: A rose is a woody perennial flowering plant. There are over a hundred species in the genus rosa. Oil from roses can be used as perfumes.

Rue

Kingdom	Order	Family	Genus
Plantae	Sapindales	Rutaceae	Ruta

Native Region: Mediterranean and southwest Asia.

Features: The leaves have a green, feathery appearance. The flower petals are yellow. Rue has a distinctive bitter taste.

Magical Properties: Healing and poison antidote.

Details: Rue, also known as common rue, or herb-of-grace is an evergreen shrub. Getting rue on your skin can cause allergic reactions. Cats dislike rue while caterpillars prefer it.

Sage

Kingdom	Order	Family	Genus
Plantae	Lamiales	Lamiaceae	Salvia

Native Region: Mediterranean.

Features: Comes in a variety of sizes and colors. They are most commonly associated with lavender flowers that have oval leaves.

Magical Properties: Wards off dark magic.

Details: Salvia officianalis has many names, including common sage, garden sage, golden sage kitchen sage and true sage. In best conditions sage can grow to 1 meter squared and in cold weather sage will easily expire.

Scurvy Grass

Kingdom	Order	Family	Genus
Plantae	Brassicales	Brassicaceae	Cochlearia

Native Region: Europe.

Features: Low, rounded or creeping plants, up to 20 cm tall. Multiple small flowers decorate the stem.

Magical Properties: Inflaming the brain.

Details: Cochlearia officinalis, or scurvy grass is a biennial herb that grows in salt marshes or along the seashore. Its high vitamin C content meant is was used in the past to help cure or prevent scurvy, or vitamin C deficiency. Scurvy grass also has antiseptic, diuretic and mild laxative properties.

Shrivelfigs

Kingdom	Order	Family	Genus
Magicae Plantae	Rosales	Moraceae	Ficticus

Native Region: Ethiopia

Features: The flowers of the shrivelfig grow inside the fruit, both of which are purple in color. When skinned, the fruit (which is actually the plant's flower and contains blossoms inside) produces a purple liquid.

Magical Properties: Joy, comfort and euphoria.

Details: It's a deciduous plant, meaning that its leaves start to shed in autumn and the plant is leafless during winter. However, due to its aggressive roots, the plant can still survive even in snowy conditions.

Silverweed

Kingdom	Order	Family	Genus
Plantae	Rosales	Rosaceae	Argentina

Native Region: Northern hemisphere.

Features: Red stolon with green leaves and white undersides. The yellow flowers grow from a single green stem.

Magical Properties: Used in alchemy to change objects into metal.

Details: Argentina anserina, or silverweed, is a perennial flowering plant.

Snakeweed

Kingdom	Order	Family	Genus
Plantae	Asterales	Asteraceae	Guiterrezia

Native Region: North America.

Features: Green or brown stems with a woody base. Yellow flowers with an oval fruit, covered in scales.

Magical Properties: Cure for colds, coughs and respiratory issues.

Details: Gutierrezia sarothrae, also known as snakeweed, is commonly confused with rabbitbrush but is distinguished by the presence of ray flowers. It is toxic to domestic sheep, goats, and cattle when consumed in large quantities.

Sneezewort

Kingdom	Order	Family	Genus
Plantae	Asterales	Asteraceae	Achillea

Native Region: Europe.

Features: Loose clusters of white flower heads. Its leaves are dark green.

Magical Properties: Inflaming the brain. The dried leaves can induce sneezing or ward off bugs.

Details: Achillea ptarmico is an herbaceous perennial flowering plant. It is a hardy, drought tolerant plant that prefers full sun and moist soil. It is poisonous to livestock.

Sopophorous Bean

Kingdom	Order	Family	Genus
Magicae Plantae	Fabales	Fabaceae	Sopopoperus

Native Region: Central America.

Features: Shriveled, pearly-white bean which contains a thick silver juice.

Magical Properties: The juice will remove the drinker's memory. The bean will render someone unconscious.

Details: The sopophorous bean is a legume that is somewhat unknown in its native region of Central America because it hides deep in the ground. It can only be harvested with the accio charm, which prevents muggles from finding it.

Spleenwart

Kingdom	Order	Family	Genus
Plantae	Polypodiales	Aspleniaceae	Asplenium

Native Region: North America and South Africa.

Features: Reddish-brown stem and leaf axis.

Magical Properties: Allows sight of invisible people or objects.

Details: Asplenium platyneuron, or spleenwart, grows in a wide variety of habitats, growing both on rocks and soil.

Squill

Kingdom	Order	Family	Genus
Plantae	Asparagales	Asparagaceae	Drimia

Native Region: Southern Europe, western Asia and northern Africa.

Features: Rosettes of meter long green leave grows from large brownish bulbs. In the fall it produces plentiful little white flowers.

Magical Properties: Makes potions warm and smooth to drink.

Details: Drimia maritima, also known as squill or sea onion, is a flowering plant. It has a bitter taste and is very poisonous.

St John's Wort

Kingdom	Order	Family	Genus
Plantae	Malpighiales	Hypericaceae	Hypericum

Native Region: Europe and Asia.

Features: Green, oval leaves sprout directly from an upright stem.

Magical Properties: Healing and mood altering.

Details: Hypericum perforatum, also known as St. John's Wort is an herbaceous perennial plant named for traditionally being harvested on St. John's Day, June 24th.

Staghorn

Kingdom	Order	Family	Genus
Fungi	Xylariales	Xylariaceae	Xylaria

Native Region: Tropical South America and Africa.

Features: A small fungus with a tough texture. The fruit body is cylindrical in twisting shapes similar in appearance to antlers.

Magical Properties: Healing and growth inhibitor.

Details: Xylaria hypoxylon, or staghorn, grows in groups on decaying wood.

Star Grass

Kingdom	Order	Family	Genus
Plantae	Asparagales	Hyposidaceae	Hypoxis

Native Region: South Africa.

Features: Green upright stem with yellow teacup flowers.

Magical Properties: Healing and soothing injuries.

Details: Hypoxis is a perennial herb that grows across the grasslands of Africa. This has earned it the additional name of the African Potato. The flavor of the flower is described as "a little sour."

Starthistle

Kingdom	Order	Family	Genus
Plantae	Asterales	Asteraceae	Centaurae

Native Region: Mediterranean.

Features: A weedy plant with spiny leaves and flowers of blue or purple petals.

Magical Properties: Reduction or removal of growths on or in the body.

Details: Centaurar, also known as starthistle, knapweeds, loggerheads and centaury, are herbaceous flowering plants. Though pleasant looking, starthistle is a weed that can grow uncontrollably. Starthistle attracts pests.

Stinging Nettle

Kingdom	Order	Family	Genus
Plantae	Rosales	Urticaceae	Urtica

Native Region: Europe, Asia, northern Africa, and western North America.

Features: It can grow to 2 meters (about 7 feet) in the summer, sprouting green, hairy leaves with multiple sharp, pointed ridges.

Magical Properties: Fresh stinging nettles are used to strengthen healing potions while dried nettles are used to strengthen poisonous potions.

Details: Urtica dioica, also known as the stinging nettle or nettle leaf, is an herbaceous, perennial plant. It is usually found in the countryside and the sole food source for a number of butterfly species.

Sunflower

Kingdom	Order	Family	Genus
Plantae	Asterales	Asteraceae	Helianthus

Native Region: North America.

Features: The stem can grow up to 3 meters (almost 10 feet). The flowers are bright yellow with a center of florets.

Magical Properties: Creates radiating joy, gladness and jubilation.

Details: Helianthus annuus, or sunflower, is a perennial plant which spreads swiftly and is invasive to other plants. During growth, sunflowers will tilt toward the sun over the course of each day.

Thyme

Kingdom	Order	Family	Genus
Plantae	Lamiales	Lamiaceae	Thymus

Native Region: Europe, Asia and northern Africa.

Features: Small flowers growing in clumps of hundreds with very narrow stems of yellow, white or purple flowers.

Magical Properties: Thyme helps to cure a variety of common ailments such as diarrhea, stomach ache, cough, bronchitis and flatulence.

Details: Perennial evergreen herb that is aromatic. There are about 350 species of thyme. Thyme is a popular herb for cooking as well.

Tormentil

Kingdom	Order	Family	Genus
Plantae	Rosales	Rosaceae	Potentilla

Native Region: Northern Europe, northern Asia and North America.

Features: Some species may have stems with 3 leaves connected at one point while others may have 15 or more leaves. The flowers are typically yellow but may be white, pink or red. The fruit is dry and inedible.

Magical Properties: Inhibit or cease flight in flying magical creatures.

Details: Potentilla, also known as tormentil, barren strawberry or cinquefoils represents over 300 species of plants in the rose family. These can be herbaceous perennials, shrubs or even weeds. This plant is a favorite amongst caterpillars.

Umbrella Palm

Kingdom	Order	Family	Genus
Plantae	Arecales	Arecaceae	Hedyscepe

Native Region: Lord Howe Island in Australia.

Features: A slow-growing palm with a slender trunk, prominent silvery crownshaft and a compact crown of dense, dark green, stiffly arching fronds.

Magical Properties: Concentrated fruit provides excess energy. However, if the fruit floats in water, the opposite occurs with a long-lasting effect of lethargy.

Details: Hedyscepe, or the umbrella palm, has egg sized fruits that take up to four years to ripen and it is not easy to tell when the seeds are ripe. The palms do not form annual tree rings. It grows on mountain forests, cliffs and exposed ridges overlooking the sea.

Valerian

Kingdom	Order	Family	Genus
Plantae	Dispacales	Caprifoliaceae	Valeriana

Native Region: Europe.

Features: Sweetly scented pink or white flowers blooming in multiple bunches from small branches aligning the soft stem.

Magical Properties: Causes sleep or unconsciousness and is used as a sedative.

Details: Valeriana officinalis, or all-heal, is a perennial flowering plant. The actual effect of the plant is central nervous system depression which causes sleep to occur. Valerian attracts cats and it is also considered an invasive species (weed) and is thus banned in many areas around the world such as in some US cities and parts of the United Kingdom.

Wartizome

Kingdom	Order	Family	Genus
Magicae Plantae	Malpighiales	Hypericaceae	Zoma

Native Region: Europe and Asia.

Features: Green, oval leaves sprout directly from the stem. The flower is a purple colored bulb which droops from its weight.

Magical Properties: Depressant, sedative and calmative.

Details: Watizone is an herbaceous perennial plant that is found in forests with sparse light. The plant grows in the shadows and will wilt within the first day of being picked, although its bulb will remain magically potent for a long time.

Watercress

Kingdom	Order	Family	Genus
Plantae	Brassicales	Brassicaceae	Nasturtium

Native Region: Europe and Asia.

Features: Hollow green stems with oval leaves which floats on the surface of water. The white flowers grow in small clusters.

Magical Properties: Cleansing and detoxifying.

Details: Nasturtium officinale, or watercress, is an aquatic plant and as such is 95% water. It has a distinct peppery flavor and is a favorite of hoverflies.

Wiggentree

Kingdom	Order	Family	Genus
Plantae	Rosales	Ulmaceae	Finis

Native Region: Northern Europe.

Features: The wiggentree grows wonderfully tall with lush almond shaped leaves and a vibrant brown trunk.

Magical Properties: The bark of the tree repels dark creatures.

Details: The wiggentree is a magical rowan that will protect anyone touching its trunk from the attack of dark creatures. The wiggentree is guarded by bowtruckles. Closely related is the wiggenbush which, although much shorter, has similar magical characteristics.

Winterberry

Kingdom	Order	Family	Genus
Plantae	Aquifoliales	Aquifoliaceae	Ilex

Native Region: Eastern North America.

Features: Grows in a dense thicket with leaves that are glossy green and serrated. Flowers are small with five to eight white petals. Round red fruit forms in a bunch and is highly toxic as are the leaves.

Magical Properties: The berries can be used to cast a transparent protective shield around the user. Close proximity to the wood can calm those with a temper.

Details: Illex verticillate, or winterberry, is one of 500 species of holly. Its fruit ripens in the winter and the bare branches are exposed. Winterberry grows best in acidic soil of wetland habitats. Its wood is also harvested for wands that are intended to be used in wintry climates.

Witch's Ganglion

Kingdom	Order	Family	Genus
Magicae Plantae	Asterales	Asteraceae	Hecatus

Native Region: China.

Features: It has a distinctive blood-red bulb that throbs.

Magical Properties: Rare and unknown.

Details: Witch's ganglion is endemic to the Far East, and grows on ponds. It is of some rarity, since knowledge of it in the Western world is limited to anecdotes of wizards who journeyed East and encountered it.

Wormwood

Kingdom	Order	Family	Genus
Plantae	Asterales	Asteraceae	Artemisia

Native Region: Temperate Europe, Asian and northern Africa.

Features: The stems are tall and straight with grooved branches. The leaves are greenish-grey with a white underside; the leaves along the stem are shorter than those towards the base. The flowers are a light yellow with drooping heads.

Magical Properties: Removes side effects from other ingredients. A side effect of this ingredient may be hallucinations.

Details: Artemisia absinthium, or wormwood, is an herbaceous, perennial plant. The herb is very bitter and grows best under bright light.

Yarrow

Kingdom	Order	Family	Genus
Plantae	Asterales	Asteraceae	Achillia

Native Region: Northern Asia, northern Europe and North America.

Features: Leaves are evenly distributed along the stem with varying degrees of hairiness. The plant has a strong, sweet scent with white to pink flowers.

Magical Properties: Fire resistance and healing of burns.

Details: Blossoms and root are chewed, then the juice is applied topically before approaching fire. A poultice of the pulverized plant can be mixed with water and used to treat burns.

Yellow Staghorn

Kingdom	Order	Family	Genus
Fungi	Dacrymycetes	Dacrymycetaceae	Calocera

Native Region: Scotland.

Features: It has multiple bright orange, branching arms with a soft, rubbery texture.

Magical Properties: Healing and nullifies growth effects.

Details: Calocera viscosa, also known as yellow staghorn or jelly fungus, grows on decaying conifer trees.

Zebrawood

Kingdom	Order	Family	Genus
Plantae	Sapindales	Anacardiaceae	Astronium

Native Region: Central and South America.

Features: The heartwood, found under the bark, is a pale golden yellow with variable width strips of medium to dark brown. The timber becomes darker after exposure to air and the stripes become nearly black.

Magical Properties: Disguise and confusion.

Details: The wood is very tough and durable. It is resistant to bugs and fungi. Because of its hardness, the wood smolders for a long time when burned and emits black and white smoke.

Section 2

Potion Ingredients

Agrippa

Type: Mineral

Description: Agrippa causes skepticism and disbelief in the subject, which makes it an ideal ingredient for muggle misdirection.

Antimony

Type: Chemical

Description: Antimony (chemical symbol: Sb) is a silvery white, crystalline solid used for fire resistance.

Aqua Vitæ

Type: Mineral

Description: Known as "water of life," this ethanol causes recklessness and poor judgement.

Armadillo

Type: Animal Kingdom

Description: Armadillo produce a bile that aides in focus and alertness.

Asian Dragon

Type: Animal Kingdom

Description: Asian dragon hair makes a potion stiff and inflexible.

Bat

Type: Animal Kingdom

Description: Bat spleen can be added to a potion to breakdown the composition of other ingredients.

Bicorn

Type: Animal Kingdom

Description: Bicorns possess two large horns that are shed annually. Powdered horn is used to reform atoms after a transfiguration.

Black Beetle

Type: Animal Kingdom

Description: Beetle eyes are a common potion ingredient used as a magical base to allow other ingredients to mix with water.

Billywig

Type: Animal Kingdom

Description: The sting of the billywig has the ability to make a person float off the ground. The sting produces a slime with curative properties.

Blatta Pulvereus

Type: Animal Kingdom

Description: A type of cockroach, can be used in potions to help dissolve hard ingredients such as bones.

Blowfly

Type: Animal Kingdom

Description: Blowfly can be added to a potion to mask some stronger flavors, although the flavor of the blowfly is not particularly desirable itself.

Boomslang

Type: Mineral

Description: Boomslang skin is used in multi-step potions to complete the prior stages of preparation in order to retain the magical effect achieved up to that point.

Bulbadox

Type: Mineral

Description: As a juice or a powder, buldabox causes boils.

Bundimun

Type: Animal Kingdom

Description: Bundimun secretion or ooze is an acidic substance that can rot a building's structure. When diluted it can break down spills and stains without destroying the object being cleaned.

Camphirated Spirit

Type: Mineral

Description: A distilled liquid form of camphor, it has disinfectant properties, and is used to clean wounds.

Cat

Type: Animal Kingdom

Description: Cat hair in a potion can make the subject astute, clever and quick.

Caterpillar

Type: Animal Kingdom

Description: A caterpillar used in a proper potion can cause the subject to shrink or shrivel.

Chizpurfle

Type: Animal Kingdom

Description: The carapace of the Chizpurfle is used as an antidote to poison and other ingredients. Chizpurfle fangs cause startled and altered feelings.

Clabbert

Type: Animal Kingdom

Description: A clabbert pustule, located on the forehead, flashes red whenever the creature senses danger and can pass this skill in a potion.

Cockroach

Type: Animal Kingdom

Description: A cockroach is able to withstand many of the effects of other potion ingredients so it is used to create a paste without diluting the potion's effects.

Croakoa

Type: Mineral

Description: Croakoa causes hopping and a frog like "croak" to come from the imbued object.

Crocodile

Type: Animal Kingdom

Description: The heart of a crocodile causes the subject's tear ducts to dry up which stops the production of tears.

Doxy

Type: Animal Kingdom

Description: Doxy venom causes hyperactivity. Doxy eggs are also often used as a less potent version of the venom.

Dragon

Type: Animal Kingdom

Description: Dragon claws, horns and livers are used for fire resistance and rejuvenation qualities.

Dragonfly

Type: Animal Kingdom

Description: Dragonfly thorax increases the subject's stamina to increase the length of time it can withstand physical exertion.

Eagle Owl

Type: Animal Kingdom

Description: Eagle owl feathers increase the body temperature of the subject. This change can be dangerous in humans so this ingredient is most often used with beats.

Eel

Type: Animal Kingdom

Description: Eel eyes cause the subject to have their own eye's swell and bug out.

Erumpent

Type: Animal Kingdom

Description: The horn erumpet contains a deadly fluid that causes whatever it is injected into to explode.

Fairy

Type: Animal Kingdom

Description: The wings of the fairy are used to cast an aura around the subject which helps retain the effects of other ingredients.

Flabberghasted Leech

Type: Animal Kingdom

Description: Flabberghasted leeches causes surprise and astonishment.

Flitterby

Type: Animal Kingdom

Description: The flitterby is a moth with orange glowing wings who hum lightly and playfully when in flight. Used in a potion they cause a sense of airiness and carefree feelings.

Flobberworm

Type: Animal Kingdom

Description: The mucus from the Flobberworm is sometimes used to thicken potions.

Flying Seahorses

Type: Animal Kingdom

Description: Flying Seahorses gives extra endurance and fortitude.

Frog

Type: Animal Kingdom

Description: The secretion of frogs can cause a wide variety of magical effects from healing to poison.

Giant Purple Toad

Type: Animal Kingdom

Description: Giant purple toads are a favorite food of dragons and are typically added to dragon potions to increase the possibility of a dragon properly taking the potion.

Glumbumble

Type: Animal Kingdom

Description: The treacle produced by the glumbumble acts as an antidote to the hysteria effects of Alihotsy leaves.

Gnat

Type: Animal Kingdom

Description: Gnat heads are used to suppress strong emotions like jealousy and hate.

Goat

Type: Animal Kingdom

Description: A stone (undigested clumps of matter) taken from the stomach of a goat is called a bezoar and can be used to counteract most poisons.

Graphorn

Type: Animal Kingdom

Description: Graphorn horn is highly prized as a potion ingredient used to give an invisible shield of protection around the subject.

Griffin

Type: Animal Kingdom

Description: Griffin claws, when powdered, can be used as an ingredient to increase strength.

Haliwinkles

Type: Animal Kingdom

Description: Haliwinkles can be used to fend of feelings of nausea or sea sickness.

Honeywater

Type: Mineral

Description: Honeywater is a solution of honey diluted in water which can coat the drinkers throat to protect against pain such as a sore throat.

Horklump

Type: Animal Kingdom

Description: Horklump juice is a substance extracted from horklumps. It can be used in a range of healing potions.

Horned Slug

Type: Animal Kingdom

Description: Horned slugs are a type of a slug that, when stewed, heals skin irritations such as pimples or boils.

Horned Toad

Type: Animal Kingdom

Description: The horned toad causes inflammation or bloating in the body.

Horse Hair

Type: Animal Kingdom

Description: Horse hair can slightly increase the speed and strength of the subject.

Jobberknoll

Type: Animal Kingdom

Description: The feather of the Jobberknoll is used to enhance the subject's memory of past events. This is also useful in the highly regulated truth serum to help the subject remember past facts they are asked to tell.

Knarl

Type: Animal Kingdom

Description: Knarl quills cause the subject to faint but only remain unconscious for a brief period of time.

Lacewing Fly

Type: Animal Kingdom

Description: Stewed lacewing flies are used to make a base for complex potions. Lacewing flies usually have to stew for a long period before becoming usable as a magical ingredient.

Leech

Type: Animal Kingdom

Description: Leeches and leech juice can lengthen the time of the effect of the potion it is used in.

Lethe River Water

Type: Mineral

Description: Lethe river water, collected from the river Lethe causes one to forget things.

Lionfish

Type: Animal Kingdom

Description: Lionfish have extremely long and serrated spines. Crushed into a powder, these spines can be used in healing or to ward off dark magic.

Lobalug

Type: Animal Kingdom

Description: The venom of the Lobalug is a defensive mechanism employed by the creature to deter attackers and can be used as a protective ingredient.

Mars

Type: Mineral

Description: Also known as iron (chemical symbol: Fe) can be used to increase the use of oxygen in most any subject. It is often seen on a lesser level in dietary iron such as red meats, beans and certain vegetables.

Mercury

Type: Mineral

Description: Mercury (chemical symbol: Sb) is a poisonous liquid, used to gauge temperatures.

Moonstone

Type: Mineral

Description: Moonstone (also known as the wishing stone) is a gemstone. Powdered moonstone has a calming and peaceful effect.

Morning dew

Type: Mineral

Description: Morning dew, also simply known as dew, is water that collects on the leaves of plants in the early morning due to condensation. The ingredient increases the sense of purity and cleanliness.

Murtlap

Type: Animal Kingdom

Description: A Murtlap tentacle is a rare potion ingredient that gives a heightened resistance to curses and jinxes. An overdose has the side effect of purple ear hair.

Newt

Type: Animal Kingdom

Description: Newt's eyes are used as a poison. The spleen is used to filter some negative effects from other ingredients.

Occamy

Type: Animal Kingdom

Description: The egg of the occamy is made of pure silver and has luster-giving properties.

Octopus

Type: Animal Kingdom

Description: Octopus powder, made from the dried flesh of an octopus, increases the strength of potions.

Peacock

Type: Animal Kingdom

Description: Peacock feathers can increase the flight ability of creatures that can already fly.

Pearl

Type: Mineral

Description: Pearl dust creates a strong sense of attraction which makes it a prime ingredient in love potions,

Plimpy

Type: Animal Kingdom

Description: Plimpy eyes are use as fertilizer.

Porcupine

Type: Animal Kingdom

Description: Porcupine quills are used as an anesthesia to remove painful effects of other ingredients.

Puffskein

Type: Animal Kingdom

Description: A puffskein is covered in soft fur which causes a tickling sensation and laughing.

Ptolemy

Type: Mineral

Description: Ptolemy is a blood-red poison.

Rat

Type: Animal Kingdom

Description: Rat spleen causes a subject to shrink in size while rat tails are used to make hair follicles stand on end.

Re'em

Type: Animal Kingdom

Description: Re'em blood gives the drinker immense strength for a short time, making it a highly desired substance.

Runespoor

Type: Animal Kingdom

Description: Powdered runespoor fangs can assist in apparition while runespoor eggs have the ability to increase the mental agility of the drinker.

Salamander

Type: Animal Kingdom

Description: Salamander blood increases the durability of the subject, allowing them to take on rigorous tasks without physical harm.

Salt

Type: Mineral

Description: Salt, also known as table salt or rock salt, is used as a preservative with the salt of the African Sea being considered one of the most magically potent preservatives.

Saltpetre

Type: Mineral

Description: Saltpetre is another name for the mineral form of potassium nitrate and is used to preserve or protect the body during transfiguration.

Scarab Beetle

Type: Animal Kingdom

Description: Ground scarab beetles are used to increase concentration.

Shrake

Type: Animal Kingdom

Description: The spines of the shrake can be used to stabilize ingredients of a potion used for healing.

Sloth

Type: Animal Kingdom

Description: Sloth's brains cause the subject to become languid and slow.

Snake

Type: Animal Kingdom

Description: Snake fangs from non-venomous snakes creates alertness and attentiveness in the subject.

Spider

Type: Animal Kingdom

Description: Most types of spiders cause a sneaky or stealthy effect in the subject.

Standard Ingredient

Type: Mineral/Chemical

Description: The standard ingredient is an herb which was classically used by witches and wizards through the ages in their potions, thus the title. It strengthens any negative effects cause by other ingredients.

Streeler

Type: Animal Kingdom

Description: Streelers are toxic and used to disperse the most stubborn of creatures or beasts.

Tar

Type: Mineral

Description: Tar is a dark, thick, flammable substance produced through the distillation of wood or coal. It is too strong of an ingredient for human use but can be useful in healing or binding beasts.

Tartar

Type: Mineral

Description: Tartar causes burping or belching in the subject.

Tubeworm

Type: Animal Kingdom

Description: Tubeworms are a general group of any worm-like aquatic creatures that secrete a mineral tube around their body. They can be used to give night vision but may have the side effect of causing nightmares.

Unicorn

Type: Animal Kingdom

Description: Unicorn tail hair is used to cause feelings of awe and wonderment.
Unicorn horn is a strong healing ingredient used to restore and cure.

Venomous Tentacula

Type: Animal Kingdom

Description: Venomous tentacula creates a strong internal burning sensation which is excruciatingly painful to humans but can be used to strengthen some beasts, such as dragons. It may also turn one's skin purple.

Vitriol

Type: Mineral

Description: Vitriol is a highly corrosive acid and creates holes within the subject.

Wartcap

Type: Mineral

Description: Wartcap powder causes the skin of a person who touches it to form a thick hard crust which protects from low level damage and is fire resistant.

White Spirit

Type: Mineral

Description: White spirit is clear liquid derived from paraffin that is commonly used as a solvent in painting. It was an ingredient in a curative solution used to treat scale rot in dragons, along with salt water and tar.

Wood Louse

Type: Animal Kingdom

Description: Woodlice can add a slight increase to the effects of potion ingredients but if combined with too many other ingredients it will nullify the potions effects.

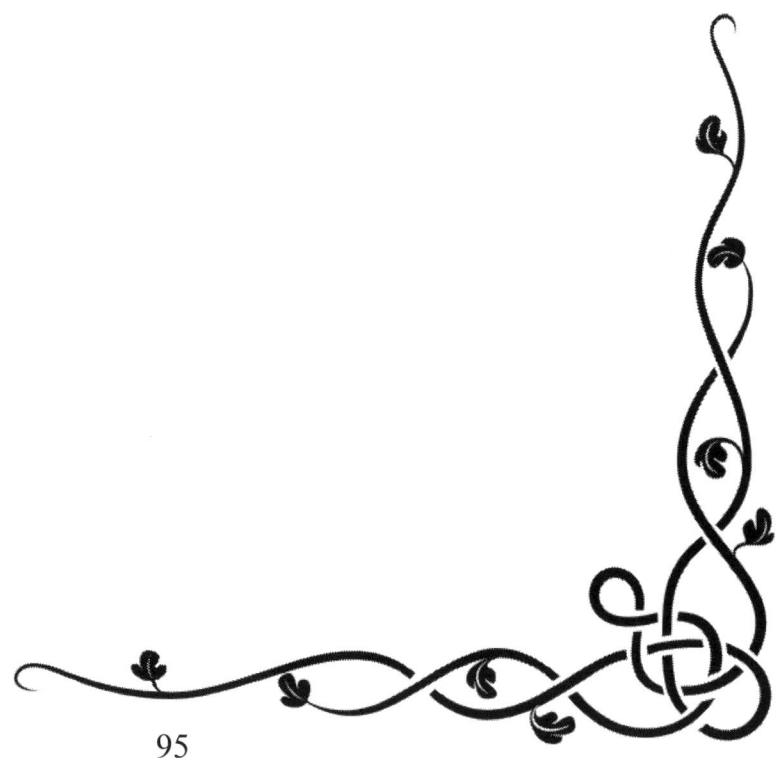

Printed in Great Britain
by Amazon